The Narrowing Road

14 Crossings with Bashō

George Myers Jr.

Sandy Press

The Narrowing Road: 14 Crossings with Bashō

ISBN: 979-8-9949368-0-1

Printed in USA

Manufactured in the United States of America. First published as a Sandy Press paperback in 2026. Design by harry k stammer.

Sandy Press
Queensland, Australia
California, USA
sandy-press.com

Acknowledgments

My thanks to the translators whose work opened Bashō's *The Narrow Road to the Deep North* to me — Hiroaki Sato, David Landis Barnhill, and Donald Keene (the latter through Miyata Masayuki's illustrated Kodansha edition). Their care and clarity made this dialogue possible. I'm grateful as well to harry k stammer, who encouraged this small book while it was still taking shape. And to Barbara, with whom I've walked the furthest.

Contents

Introduction

Each age invents its own syntax for seeing. In ours — restless, multimedia, porous — pure forms often feel too narrow to hold what's real. Hybrid writing arises wherever boundaries fail to contain perception: prose reaching toward lyric, image bending toward silence. Long before we had a name for such crossings, Matsuo Bashō (1644–1694) traveled and wrote in two breaths — narrative and pause — creating a hybrid rhythm of attention that feels uncannily modern.

Bashō's life was shaped by movement. Born Matsuo Kinsaku and trained in the samurai tradition, he left behind both status and security when he devoted himself to poetry. He eventually settled in a modest hut along the Sumida River, where the broad leaves of a banana plant — *bashō* — brushed the walls and gave him the name he carried forward.

Life there wasn't isolated in the romantic sense. Edo was a crowded, restless capital. Students and visitors came and went; poems were exchanged almost daily. Yet something in Bashō leaned toward distance — toward the discipline of walking, of lightness, of reducing one's possessions to what could be carried. He believed the world clarified itself when the body entered it without the defenses of comfort or excess intention.

In 1689 he undertook his longest walk: the journey that became *Oku no Hosomichi (The Narrow Road to the Deep North*). His companion on the walk, Kawai Sora, was both student and friend — a quieter presence, steady in temperament, diligent in keeping notes. Their partnership complicates the usual image of the solitary wandering poet. Travel with another person creates a different kind of awareness: shared silences, negotiated pace, unspoken agreements about when to stop, when to press on, what to notice, what to leave aside. Even the aches are doubled; one person's fatigue echoes in the other.

Together they moved through regions already ancient in 1689, crossing the Shirakawa Barrier into the deep northern provinces, where history had accumulated in layers of ruin and resilience. They stood before the sacred mountains of Nikkō, walked the quiet devastation of Hiraizumi, passed plains shimmering with rice seedlings, endured storms that forced them into makeshift shelters, and contemplated the stark isolation of Sado Island rising from the sea like a dark, self-contained fate.

Their path was not linear. It was shaped by weather, by illness, by hospitality found in unlikely places, by the simple fact of two bodies navigating terrain neither had traveled before.

The strength of *The Narrow Road* lies not in revelation but in what the walk recorded: stone steps furred with moss; a horse tethered in shade; the smell of rain-soaked cedar;

the shock of ruins where a golden capital once stood. These moments endure because Bashō walked with an attentiveness, trusting that the world reveals itself in materials — not abstractions, not metaphors, but in the physical truth of things.

I came to Bashō through Donald Keene and other translators whose fidelity made my adaptations possible. They showed me that Bashō's work is not delicate; it is grounded. It holds cedar, smoke, mud, frost, hunger, fatigue, the quicksilver precision of weather, and *ma* (間), a sensitivity to silence and interval. His art was built not on concepts but on contact.

Even haiku, in his practice, begins with breath and ends in silence. In Japanese he wrote in *on* (音) — the sound-units that structure traditional haiku — and they move more lightly than English syllables. To impose a strict 17-syllable count on our slower, heavier English would stiffen what is meant to be quick and fluid. So my haiku here follow Bashō's pattern, not inherited arithmetic: short–long–short; breath–turn–silence. Cadence over counting. Movement over rule.

What follows in this book is not translation. It is conversation — a parallel walk taken three centuries later, shaped by the materials of my own life: the rasp of ditch weeds in a crosswind; the hollow knock of a boot on a culvert; dust rising from a long-unused road; the tug in the knee announcing its limits. Bashō's haibun stand on the left-hand page, the initiating breath of each crossing, with mine on the right. In this design, the spine becomes a literal narrow road, the white interior margin forming a shared corridor of attention. The idea is to listen to the path and Bashō and talk with when talk is called for — not to talk over, not to compete.

From among Bashō's haibun from his walk, I revisit 14 — those that resonate most strongly with modern thresholds, with our unsettled and searching century. Notes at the end offer historical grounding, but the haibun themselves are left unencumbered, as Bashō intended.

I've written my own pieces as a tuning in noticing. Entering into dialogue with his journeys became a way of relearning attention — small, patient, deliberate. If this book offers anything, I hope it offers a brief slackening in today's noisy rush: a way of seeing that steadies rather than accelerates, as if someone were walking beside you for a while.

These pieces are crossings: between poems and prose; between centuries; between two companions moving through different landscapes with the same attentive gait; between what endures and what falls away; between two narrowing roads held, briefly, together through the book's spine.

1. 行く春 — Yuku Haru

Bashō

The months and days are travelers of eternity; the passing years, too, come and go like wanderers. Many people drift through life on boats; others grow old while leading their horses down long roads. For such people, each day is a journey, and the journey becomes their home. Even in ancient times, countless travelers met their final moments away from familiar places.

As spring passed this year, I found myself restless once more. The way birds cry and fish seem to glisten with tears made the season's departure feel heavy. I mended my worn sleeves, tightened the ties of my traveling robe, and arranged the few things I could carry. Then, entrusting my body to the road, I set out — my heart already moving ahead of my steps.

Departing spring —
birds crying,
fish eyes wet

Departing Spring (Yuku Haru)

Spring changes in the body before it changes in the world. I wake with a stiffness that feels borrowed, as if someone older has loaned me their morning. The light coming through the blinds is too thin to trust; my balance felt a half second behind me. The floorboards hesitated before responding to my weight.

Outside, the street holds a faint shimmer from last night's rain. A garbage can left on its side leaks a slow thread of water that worms toward the storm drain. A single glove lies in the middle of the road — child-sized, red — positioned as if someone set it there to mark a fault line. I step around it without knowing why it unsettles me.

Nothing in my life is in motion, yet things feel on the verge of shifting. The season's leaving exposes whatever I've kept tucked at the edges. It's the sense that if I remain exactly as I am, something vital will harden.
So I move. One deliberate step. Then another. Because walking still fits.

Departing spring —
my shadow loosens
before I do

2. 白河の関 — Shirakawa no Seki

Bashō

When we reached the ancient barrier of Shirakawa, the long journey behind us seemed to fall suddenly silent. The old checkpoint stood with its posts leaning, half-buried in earth and softened by moss. The path around it was overgrown, and the stone markers that once guided travelers now lay scattered, worn nearly smooth by the years.

Even so, something in the air felt unmistakable — the sense that this boundary carried the weight of many departures.

For generations, poets and wanderers had paused here, leaving behind verses and stories, and as I stepped forward I felt the old longing rise within me. The wind moved across the barrier with a faint rustle, as if brushing through the traces of those earlier footprints. I stood for a moment, unsure whether I was entering the deep north or being received by it.

Among deutzia blooms —
the Shirakawa Barrier
comes into view

Shirakawa Barrier (Shirakawa no Seki)

Crossing into a different life requires a quiet audit of the one you're leaving. I felt it before I reached the edge of town: a pressure at the base of the throat, a pulse of doubt that didn't let go. I felt it in the left knee before I felt it in the air.

The place itself was nothing dramatic — gravel, a sagging fence, a utility pole humming with a faint electrical tremor. But the worn edges carried a leftover severity. The kind of spot where arguments have ended or begun. Where someone once waited too long for someone.

I paused. The air smelled of damp earth and old metal, the way forgotten places do when rain moves through them. No marker, no ceremony — just the sense that stepping forward meant leaving some version of myself behind. Only noticeable later.

I stepped anyway.

Fading daylight —
a fence shadow
splits the road

3. 松島 — **Matsushima**

Bashō

From Shiogama, we hired a boat to cross the inlet and make our way toward Matsushima. As we rowed out, the water widened into a great expanse, and the islands began to appear — pines growing from sheer rock, trunks twisted by sea wind, branches leaning over the tide like old friends greeting travelers. Some islands rose steeply from the waves; others barely lifted above them, shaped into curious forms as if carved by unseen hands. The boatman pointed out one after another, naming them as though introducing us to a long-established family.

The water was calm, touched only by the dip of the oars. Sea birds circled overhead, rising and falling with the same rhythm as the boat. It seemed that no matter where I looked, the islands arranged themselves into scenes beyond the skill of any painter.

The deeper we went among them, the more the heart opened with quiet astonishment, until words themselves felt too narrow to hold what the eye received.

Matsushima —
ah! Matsushima,
Matsushima!

Matsushima Bay (Matsushima)

I stood at the water's edge expecting coherence, but the scene was too intricate for that — islands scattered like a broken necklace. The horizon flickered as if unsure how much beauty it could hold.

I've been startled by beauty before — a painting that rearranged my teeth, a piece of music that felt like someone else remembering for me, a woman in a torn white nightie, drinking coffee in the snow — but this struck from a different angle.

The world was simply more than I was prepared for.

Late tide,
rocks glint — it was
pistachio

4. 日光 — Nikkō

Bashō

The road to Nikkō rises steadily from deep forests. Ancient cedars stand so tall and close together that the light filters between them in narrow bands, and the air under their branches feels as if it has been resting there for centuries. As we climbed, the distant sound of rushing water echoed faintly among the trunks, guiding us upward like a hidden companion.

When we reached the precincts of the shrine, the buildings appeared slowly through the shade — pillars lacquered in color, carvings worked with exquisite care, roofs layered in dark, glistening tiles. Though constructed by human hands, they seemed shaped by the mountains themselves, as if the spirits of this place had long awaited their form. Even the simplest ornament on a beam felt touched by reverence.

I stepped toward the main hall and found myself overcome, not by grandeur, but by the stillness that held everything together — from the moss at the base of the trees to the distant peaks standing watch beyond the gate. To behold such harmony between craft and landscape was to understand why generations of travelers had sought this sacred ground.

How deeply sacred —
new leaves, young leaves
in the day's light

Sacred Mountains (Nikkō)

Elevation changes the mind before the view does. As the road climbed, the air thinned into something sharper, almost medicinal. Trees stood in disciplined rows; the light between them felt earned, not given.

At the crest, structures emerged from shadow: beams darkened by weather, steps furred with moss, a rail cold enough to sting my fingers. Nothing pristine — everything carrying the long patience of being repaired and repaired again. I rested my hand on a post smoothed by countless others and felt its spent authority.

A calm opened in me — not revelation, but recognition.

Mountain dusk —
the cold grain
under my palm

5. 平泉 — **Hiraizumi**

Bashō

We reached Hiraizumi toward evening. Once, this had been a city of unmatched splendor, the seat of three proud generations of lords whose wealth and power were said to rival the capital itself. Yet now almost nothing remained. The grand halls had collapsed into earth; the foundations lay scattered in the grass; only a few stones hinted at what had once stood here. The wind moved freely through the ruins, stirring the young leaves that grew where polished floors once comforted lamplight.

I climbed the hill to the site of the old palace. The plain stretched out before me, quiet and without ornament, and I found myself thinking of the fleeting rise and fall of all human affairs. Warriors who had shaped this land with their valor were now only names in the histories. The vibrant capital that had dazzled so many had vanished as thoroughly as a dream on waking.

Standing there, I felt the weight of time settle across the field, and my heart could do nothing but surrender to its solitude.

Summer grasses —
all that remains
of warriors' dreams

Ruins of Hiraizumi

Ruins never feel ancient; they feel immediate, as if collapse is always contemporary. A few stones, grass thinning over buried lines, sunlight falling unevenly across what once stood. Power imagines permanence; time says no.

A fragment of foundation jutted at an angle, smoothed in some places, severely eroded in others, and sharp-edged.

Nothing to mourn — everything to notice. Standing there, I felt how quickly the structures in a life soften back into the ground.

Evening grasses —
a buried stone
still holding its edge

6. 田植うた — Taue-uta

Bashō

The road led us down into a broad plain where the early summer fields were bright with water. Farmers stood in long rows, planting young rice shoots one by one, their motions steady and precise. Their sleeves were tied back, straw hats casting soft shadows across their faces as they bent to their work. The seedlings made faint ripples as they were pressed into the flooded earth, and the field shimmered as though stitched together by countless small movements.

From one row to the next, the voices of the planters rose in unison. The songs began as simple calls — short phrases exchanged across the water. But soon they gathered into a rhythmic chorus that carried over the fields. The sound was neither loud nor hurried; it was the measured breath of labor done together. Watching from the path, I felt the weight of the journey fall away, replaced by the quiet strength of the scene before me. In that moment, the harmony of voices and water seemed to hold the whole season.

Gathering seedlings —
the hands returning
to memories of old

Rice Planting Songs (Taue-uta)

From the road, the field sounded like steady breathing. Not a song exactly — a rhythm shaped by hands entering water, stems pressed into mud, the small slap of repetition. The water reflected a bruised sky, its surface broken with each movement.

My days rarely sync now. The field's rhythm pressed against my chest, steadying a noise I hadn't noticed I'd been carrying. Certain tasks only make sense when shared; their pace reminds you what loneliness has sped up.

A wind passed, bending the shoots in one direction, then letting them rise.

> Water field —
> voices rising
> through the sheen

7. 佐渡の浦 — Sado no ura

Bashō

From the coast we boarded a small boat to cross the stretch of water leading toward Sado, the island long known for exile and hardship. Clouds gathered heavily above the sea, and the wind pressed in from the northeast, pushing the waves into uneven ridges that rose and fell beneath the bow. The boatman worked the oar with practiced effort, calling out now and then as the current shifted. Spray touched our sleeves, cool and sharp, carrying the smell of salt and distant storms.

As we moved farther from shore, the outline of the island appeared — dark cliffs rising abruptly from the water, pines clinging to their edges, the whole shape seeming both remote and resolute. The stories of those who had been sent there echoed faintly in my mind, yet the island itself stood beyond sorrow or fear, a lonely place shaped by wind, tide, and the long drift of years. I watched the sky open above it, and for a moment the harshness of the world and the quiet endurance of the sea felt inseparable.

Rough sea —
over Sado Island
the Milky Way rises

Sado Island (Sado no Ura)

As the island came into view, the cliffs felt abrupt, the dark pines alert — as if the place had been studying us long before we saw it. For a moment I felt I was being implicated.

I shifted my footing, misjudged a slick board, and nearly stumbled over a battered pot someone had been using as a toilet. Its tilt toward me felt personal.

A lone blue boat was nodding.

The world wasn't threatening exactly — just noting that I was part of whatever story the island kept.

Offshore wind —
a loose rope
strains toward the dark

8. 荒れ宿 — Are Yado

Bashō

Night fell as we searched for a place to rest, and at last we came upon an abandoned hut standing crooked beside the road. The shutters hung loosely from their frames, and the thatched roof had been thinned by wind and rain until the rafters showed through. Inside, the floor was worn and uneven. The air carried the faint smell of damp earth. Yet even in such ruin, there was a hint of shelter — a boundary against the night, however fragile.

We set down our packs and listened to the wind slip through the gaps in the walls, bringing with it the distant cry of insects and the soft rustle of grasses brushing against the outer boards. In the dim light, the silence felt deeper for the hut's neglect, as though its emptiness had gathered all the years of travelers who once paused here.

Though it offered little comfort, I felt a quiet gratitude for the roof above us, knowing that even a broken shelter holds meaning on the long road.

In a desolate inn —
my lone body sheltering
from the rains

The Desolate Inn (Are Yado)

The structure looked abandoned before I stepped inside — roofline slumped, boards warped, a hinge hanging like it had given up on usefulness. A thin draft carried the smell of damp earth and something older.

Inside: dust drifting in uneven light, a cracked basin, a snapped handle, twine stiff with age. Nothing tragic — just remnants still performing their last tasks. The quiet carried a faint pressure, like the room was waiting to see who I'd be in it. I've lived seasons held together this way — provisional, imperfect, steady enough.

The wind tested the boards.

Broken shelter —
my breath
clouding the dark

9. 越中 — Etchū

Bashō

As we entered the province of Etchū, the sky darkened and steady rain settled in, falling without pause through the long afternoon. The road quickly softened, turning into thick mud that clung to our sandals and made each step deliberate. Water streamed down from the hillsides in thin rivulets, crossing the path and gathering in low places where boards had been laid to give travelers some footing. These planks shifted under weight, their ends darkened from seasons of storms.

The fields on either side blurred in the mist, and the outlines of distant houses appeared only faintly through the rain's pale veil. A farmer, sleeves drenched, guided an ox along the edge of a flooded paddy; the animal's slow progress matched the rhythm of the falling drops. From time to time a gust of wind rose, sending the rain slanting across our faces and rustling the reeds beside the path. Though the day was wearying, I felt a quiet acceptance in the sound of the rain — its persistence a reminder that travel unfolds in weather beyond one's choosing, each step shaped by the world as it is.

Even the young rice shoots —
as if parting tears
fall in the rain

The Road in Rain (Etchū)

Rain stripped choices to their simplest form. The road softened underfoot, boards shifting. Water ran in shallow seams, carrying leaves and grit or pooling along the way. Visibility narrowed; edges blurred.

The rain refused drama — just persistence. I pulled my jacket close knowing it wouldn't help. You can't outlast some weather.

The gray world erased the unnecessary, leaving only what contact required: step, breath, step.

Rain road —
the strap tightening
on its own

10. 乞食の庵 — Kojiki no Iori

Bashō

On the outskirts of the village we came upon a small hut, scarcely more than a few pieces of wood and thatch held together by habit and hope. It belonged to a poor beggar who had long lived there, though when we arrived he was away, seeking alms in the nearby hamlets. The place was so frail that wind slipped easily through the gaps in the walls, stirring the ashes left cold upon the earthen hearth.

A worn straw mat lay folded in one corner, its frayed edges marking years of use. Hanging from a beam was a single wooden bowl, polished smooth where hands held it countless times.

I stepped inside, feeling the uneven floor dip beneath my weight. Everything in the hut spoke of a life pared down to almost nothing, yet shaped by persistence. Even in poverty, there was a quiet order: a bundle of firewood tied neatly with rope, a patched cloth set aside to dry, a small jar placed on a flat stone to keep it steady. Standing there, I felt the dignity of the place — in the endurance that allowed it to remain standing.

Fleas, lice —
and the horse pissing
just beyond the pillow

The Beggar's Hut (Kojiki no Iori)

The hut was assembled from whatever the seasons hadn't yet taken back. Boards overlapped at odd angles, a reed mat patched a gap, a stone pinned a corner the wind kept lifting. Nothing matched; everything endured. It reminded me that I was still carrying too much.

Inside, the air held smoke and metal. A single bowl sat on a stone, rim worn smooth from years of lifting. A bundle of firewood lay tied with a frayed knot — careful in its own pared-down way. The space felt honest: no excess, no pretense.

The hut shivered once, then steadied.

Thin shelter —
a single bowl
steady on stone

11. 寺に泊る — Tera ni Tomaru

Bashō

As we entered Echizen, evening shadows lengthened across the narrow valley, and the sound of temple bells drifted faintly through the dusk. Following the path upward, we came to a small temple lodging and were welcomed to stay the night. The place was simple, built of darkened wood whose grain had been lifted by years of wind and rain. Lanterns had been hung along the veranda, their faint glow trembling in the breeze and casting soft circles of light across the worn floorboards.

Inside, the air was cool and still. A single incense stick burned in an earthen holder, its thin trail of smoke rising straight into the dim rafters. The priest brought us a bowl of clear water and set it carefully beside a wooden pillar polished smooth by the hands of countless guests.

As I rested, listening to the slow settling of the building, the deep quiet of the mountains gathered around us. Even the smallest sounds — the creak of a beam, the faint touch of wind on the shutters — felt as though they belonged to a world removed from haste.

Mountain temple —
the bell sounding softly
into evening

Temple in Echizen (*Tera ni Tomaru*)

The evening air cooled into something deliberate. The temple's wood, grain lifted by weather, smelled like rain and time. Lanterns flickered, casting tremulous rings across worn boards with more miles to put in.

Inside, silence had a temperature. Another bowl of water, this one resting near a polished pillar, its surface shifting with the building's small adjustments to night.

The quiet moved through me, loosening the noise I'd been hauling around.

Temple dusk —
cool water
holding its light

12. 山中 — Yamanaka

Bashō

The mountain path wound tightly between steep slopes, the air growing cooler as we ascended. Tall cedars crowded close on either side, their trunks rising straight into the pale morning light, and the sound of water threaded through the valley — a thin, ceaseless murmur drifting from a hidden stream. Moss covered the stones along the way, softening their sharp edges and marking where travelers had long placed their feet.

At times the trail narrowed to little more than a ledge, forcing us to move carefully as loose gravel shifted beneath our steps.

We stopped at a small hut that clung to the hillside, its roof held down by river stones and its door propped open with a piece of split bamboo. Smoke from a cooking fire drifted faintly from within, spreading the scent of damp wood. A woman offered us a drink of spring water, which she ladled from a basin carved into the earth beside the hut. As we rested, I felt how deeply the mountains held their solitude — every ridge and hollow shaped by wind, rain, and passing seasons.

Among the mountains —
water flowing
through the whole night

Among the Mountains (Yamanaka)

The trail narrowed into a rough ledge, gravel sliding just enough to make every step a negotiation. Breath scraped a little at the top of my lungs. Stones remembered storms I'd never seen.

A hut leaned into the mountain, beams bowed but bearing. A kettle dulled by decades sat on the hearth.

I touched a roof stone — cold, rough, steady — and felt the honesty of materials that don't care who you are, only how you press against them.

Ridge wind —
my pulse catching
then settling, too

13. 行く秋 — Yuku Aki

Bashō

Autumn deepened as we continued along the road, the air thinning with a quiet chill that settled into the sleeves of our traveling robes. The fields stretched pale beneath a sky already losing its heat, and the wind carried the dry scent of leaves beginning to fall. Each step felt heavier now, not only from the miles behind us, but from the season's own sense of passing. The road wound through village after village, smoke rising from hearths where families prepared for the colder nights ahead.

Along the way, I watched the shadows lengthen across the path, growing sharper and more distinct as the day declined. A lone crow called from a bare branch, its voice echoing faintly over the empty fields. The journey had worn my body thin, yet the clarity of the season brought a kind of stillness — a recognition that all things move toward their close with the same quiet inevitability. As evening drew near, the road ahead seemed both familiar and strange, stretching forward into the cool dusk.

Departing autumn —
my outstretched shadow
on the road

Toward the Journey's End (Yuku Aki)

Autumn sharpened the ground. The road speared my steps, my hip joints answering with their own small verdicts — a grind in the knee, a tug at the hips.

Ditch weeds rasped in the wind. A plank bridged a shallow washout. My boot knocked hollow against an old culvert. None of it symbolic; all of it real. The body recorded every impact.

A faint thread of woodsmoke lifted above the trees — a reminder that someone, somewhere nearby, tended warmth. I wasn't part of it, but I wasn't separate from it either. We shared the same weather. The ache aligned me with the road.

Departing autumn —
breath leaving me
visible

14. この道 — Kono Michi

Bashō

As the journey neared its close, we followed a long stretch of road that led steadily toward the plains. The land opened before us in gentle curves, the fields spreading out beneath the soft light of afternoon. Travelers passed now and then — farmers returning from work, children carrying bundles of brushwood, an old man leading a horse whose steps were slow and patient. Each moved as part of the day's quiet unfolding, unhurried and without ceremony.

Along the roadside, wild chrysanthemums bloomed in pale clusters, their leaves already touched by the season's cool breath. A small shrine stood beneath a leaning pine, its wooden offering box weathered from years of sun and rain. I paused there briefly, listening to the faint rustling of the branches overhead. The road stretched on, neither promising arrival nor marking departure, simply continuing as it always had. In that unbroken line, I felt the measure of the journey — an understanding that travel does not end with a destination, but carries forward with the world's turning.

This road —
how far it goes,
autumn evening

The Road Continues (Kono Michi)

The road leveled into a long, scuffed ribbon of dirt and broken stone — nothing scenic, just the kind of surface that answers every step with its own quiet complaint. My knees felt the miles immediately, a grind here, a tug behind an old sprain. The ache steadied me.

Fence posts leaned at irregular angles. A torn strip of tarp flickered; a hubcap flared dull light. Everything bore the marks of use, loss, continuation — materials that make sense to me.

Far off, someone hammered something metal. The sound traveled cleanly and reached me with the kind of immediacy that reminds you your life happens in a body, not a thought. Dust in the air. Cooled asphalt. Rough breath. Foot to ground, ground to bone, bone to breath. And yet.

Open road,
light widening —
footfall

Notes

The haibun that appear on the right-hand pages are my adaptations from *The Narrow Road to the Deep North*, which, over the centuries, also has been referred to as *The Narrow Road to Oku* and *The Narrow Road of the Interior.* The first English translation to use *The Narrow Road to the Deep North* appears to have been by Nobuyuki Yuasa, in the edition *Bashō: The Narrow Road to the Deep North and Other Travel Sketches* — published in 1966.

I worked from Bashō's original prose and haiku through several published translations, including those by Yuasa, Hiroaki Sato, and Donald Keene. I lightly condensed the passages to maintain the rhythm of this book and to align with the moments Bashō emphasized during his journey.

What follows is not a glossary but a brief orientation — historical, geographic, and seasonal — offered to clarify the landscapes Bashō and his friend Sora walked through, and the ones that echo through my own crossings. These notes are meant as waypoints: quiet markers at the edges of the road.

1. Departing Spring (Yuku Haru)

Bashō begins his journey at the hinge of spring and summer, a time traditionally associated with restlessness and change. The birds, fish, and passing rains mark the end of a season and the beginning of a long road. The sense of departure is both literal and interior — movement as a form of willingness.

2. Shirakawa Barrier (Shirakawa no Seki)

The barrier once marked the entrance to Japan's northern provinces. Even in Bashō's time it had fallen out of official use, but its symbolic weight remained: a threshold where travelers paused, gathered themselves, and stepped into deeper country.

3. Matsushima Bay (Matsushima)

Matsushima has long been celebrated for its pine-covered islands scattered like beads across the water. Poets often wrote that its beauty exceeded description, and Bashō's brief exclamation reflects that tradition — astonishment as wordlessness.

4. Sacred Mountains (Nikkō)

Nikkō is home to mountain shrines where architecture and landscape are fused with unusual harmony. Bashō responds less to grandeur than to the stillness held within these structures, the sense that human craft can deepen, rather than disturb, the natural world.

5. The Ruins of Hiraizumi

Once a political and cultural center, Hiraizumi was largely destroyed in the 12th century. By Bashō's arrival only scattered stones and faint foundations remained. His quiet grief reflects the Buddhist theme of impermanence: Even greatness softens back into the ground.

6. Rice Planting Songs (Taue-uta)

In early summer, teams of women planted rice in flooded fields, singing rhythmic planting songs that kept the work steady. Bashō listens to this communal breath — a harmony of labor, landscape, and season.

7. Sado Island (Sado no Ura)

This island was historically associated with exile and hardship, its cliffs rising sharply from the sea. Bashō approaches it with a mixture of awe and unease, sensing both its isolation and its endurance.

8. The Desolate Inn (Are Yado)

Roadside lodgings were often little more than provisional shelters offering minimal protection against weather. Bashō's eye falls on what remains: a roof, a boundary, a temporary refuge. Attention becomes a form of gratitude.

9. The Road in Rain (Etchū)

Travel through Etchū Province often meant continuous rain. For Bashō, rain dissolves the world into softened outlines, slowing movement and inviting acceptance — a reminder that travel unfolds in weather not of one's choosing.

10. The Beggar's Hut (Kojiki no Iori)

This fragile hut, scarcely held together, reveals a life pared down to essentials. Bashō notices the care embedded in small arrangements — a bowl, a bundle of wood — and finds dignity in persistence rather than possession.

11. Temple in Echizen (Tera ni Tomaru)

Mountain temples offered both lodging and a deeper quiet. Bashō's attention here is architectural: beams, lanterns, and the faint sound of a bell becoming part of the night's stillness.

12. Among the Mountains (Yamanaka)

The mountain paths near Yamanaka narrow into ledges bordered by cedars and running water. Bashō lingers on the solitude shaped by weather, stone, and time — solitude not as loneliness, but as clarity.

13. Toward the Journey's End (Yuku Aki)

Autumn sharpens the landscape and the body. Shadows lengthen; fields pale; the air thins. Bashō walks through this season with a heightened sense of finitude, the road aligning with his own physical limits.

14. The Road Continues (Kono Michi)

Bashō ends with a simple idea: The road does not conclude. Travel folds into continuance, and continuance requires willingness. The open path ahead carries no promise except that of being met step by step.

About the author

George Myers Jr.'s books include the poetry collection *Atmospheric Landscapes of North America*, the illustrated novella *Worlds End*, and the nonfiction books *Fast Talk with Writers* and *Mixers: On Hybrid Writing*. *Atmospheric Landscapes* and *Fast Talk* each were shortlisted for Foreword's INDIE Book of the Year. He lives in Pennsylvania.

www.ingramcontent.com/pod-product-compliance
Lightning Source LLC
LaVergne TN
LVHW091813110826
845146LV00006B/1166